I0116520

# Growing Spiritually for Teens

## Plant, Water, and Grow in God's Word

Michele Sfakianos, RN, BSN

Open Pages Publishing, LLC
http://www.openpagespublishing.com
(239) 454-7700

© 2019 Michele Sfakianos. All rights reserved. Printed and bound in the United States of America

No part of this book may be reproduced or transmitted in any form or by any means, electronic or mechanical, including photocopying, recording, or by any information storage, and retrieval system, without written permission from the author or publisher.

ISBN: (sc) 978-1-7322722-6-2

Disclaimer

The information in this book is:

- of a general nature and not intended to address the specific circumstances of a particular individual or entity;
- non-denominational;
- not gender specific; you will find instances where he/him/his is mentioned but it can also refer to she/her;
- written as a guide and is not intended to be a comprehensive tool, but is complete, accurate, or up to date at the time of writing.

# Introduction

Spiritual growth is an invitation and opportunity for all who want to follow Jesus.

When we think about how spiritual growth happens, the first thing that comes to our minds are the typical habits of going to church, prayer, reading the Bible, having quiet time, journaling, etc.

If you genuinely take God's message to heart, desire to grow in your relationship with Him, and back up that desire with action…then you will GROW in God's Word!

In this book, you will learn growing words, their definition, a short story and Bible verses.

There is a personal question in each section for you to think about. Under each question is free space for you to write or draw your answer.

Also included are "Fun facts" about the Bible that will help you to learn different meanings and terms in the Bible.

Plant yourself in God's Word, water yourself in prayer, remove any bad habits, and use everyday life as a path to grow in your relationship with Him.

# Ability

**Definition:** Possession of the means or skill to do something.

We are all born with different abilities and gifts. It is how you use those abilities and gifts that counts.

**Ecclesiastes 5:19** Moreover, when God gives someone wealth and possessions, and the ability to enjoy them, to accept their lot and be happy in their toil—this is a gift of God.

How do you enjoy the gifts God has given you? (Draw or write in the space below)

Fun fact: Luke was a Doctor.

# Alertness

**Definition:** Being aware of that which is taking place around me so I can have the right response to it.

When you are riding your bike do you stay alert to the cars around you? If you weren't alert, you could run into something. We should always stay alert to our surroundings.

**Mark 14:38** Stay awake and pray that you will not be tempted. Your spirit wants to do what is right, but your body is weak.

When are you most alert?

Fun fact: The theme of the four Gospels is the life and teaching of Jesus.

# Atonement

**Definition:** The act of making amends for sin or wrongdoing.

When you apologize for doing something wrong, that's an act of atonement. As a religious act, atonement is an effort to make up for wrongdoings so you can be in harmony with a higher power. When you atone for your sins, you are being at one with God.

**John 1:4** So be careful! Don't let the light in you become darkness.

Have you done something lately that you need to atone (make it right) for?

Fun fact: Jesus's followers were first called "Christians" in the city of Antioch.

# Attentiveness

**Definition:** Showing the worth of a person by giving undivided attention to his words and emotions.

The most valuable gift you can give someone is your time. Pay attention. When someone is talking, look them in the eye and listen to their story. They will then listen to yours.

**Hebrews 2:1** We must pay the most careful attention, therefore, to what we have heard, so that we do not drift away.

How can you give someone your undivided attention?

Fun fact: Paul wrote more books of the Bible than any other person.

# Availability

**Definition:** Making my own schedule and priorities secondary to the wishes of those I am serving.

Volunteering is a good thing. Making time in your schedule to help others makes God smile.

**Philippians 2:20-21** I have no one else like him, who will show genuine concern for your welfare. For everyone looks out for their own interests, not those of Jesus Christ.

How can you make yourself available to others?

Fun fact: Testament means covenant (contract or agreement).

# Awareness

**Definition:** Knowledge or perception of a situation or a fact.

Are you always aware of your surroundings? If you don't watch where you walk, you may fall.

**Matthew 24:50** And the master will come when the servant is not ready and is not expecting him.

Why is it easier to see in the light and not the dark?

Fun fact: We should wear all of the armor of God so that we can resist the attacks of the devil.

# Blessings

**Definition:** God's favor and protection.

Jesus walked from town to town blessing people and healing people. He taught his disciples to do the same.

**Psalms 128:2** A song for going up to worship. You will enjoy what you work for. You will be blessed with good things.

What has God blessed you with?

Fun fact: Truth is the part of Christian armor that we wear buckled around our waist.

# Boldness

**Definition:** Confidence that what I have to say or do is true and right and just in the sight of God.

To get what you want, you have to speak up. You never know if you can have something unless you ask. Be bold. Ask!

**Acts 4:29** Now, Lord, consider their threats and enable your servants to speak your word with great boldness.

How do you have boldness in the sight of God?

Fun fact: God inspired about forty people to write the Bible.

# Brave

**Definition:** Being ready to face danger; showing no fear.

Esther was challenged to be very brave. She was asked to help save God's people from a bully named Haman. Haman had an evil plan to kill all of God's people in the kingdom. Esther prayed that God would save her people, and God answered her prayer and stopped Haman's evil plan.

**Esther 4:14** You might keep quiet at this time. Then someone else will help and save the Jews. But you and your father's family will all die. And who knows, you may have been chosen queen for just such a time as this."

Is there a bully at your school? How can you show God's love by helping those who are being bullied?

Fun fact: Tabitha was raised from the dead in answer of Peter's prayer.

# Caring

**Definition:** Displaying kindness and concern for others.

At the heart of Christianity is the fact that we should be caring people. If we truly believe the Word of God, we know that apart from God, we are all headed down the wrong path.

**1 Timothy 5:4** But if a widow has children or grandchildren, the first thing they need to learn is to do their duty to their own family. When they do this, they will be repaying their parents or grandparents. That pleases God.

How do you show someone you care?

Fun fact:  Christians should rejoice always.

# Cautiousness

**Definition:** Knowing how important right timing is in accomplishing right actions.

When someone breaks a glass on the floor, aren't you careful where you walk. This is being cautious not to step on the glass.

**Proverbs 19:2** Desire without knowledge is not good—how much more will hasty feet miss the way!

How are you cautious with your actions?

Fun fact: There are sixty-six books in the Bible.

# Christian

**Definition:** A person who believes in God.

Being popular in school is a big deal. Everyone wants to be the cool kid. Many kids don't tell anyone that they are a Christian because they think they won't be cool. We should be proud of who we are. We should be proud to call ourselves Christians. We should not hide something so amazing. Instead, we should embrace God's power and share the gospel.

**Romans 1:16** I am not ashamed of the Good News. It is the power God uses to save everyone who believes - to save the Jews first, and then to save the non-Jews.

Do you think you would lose your friends if they knew you were a Christian?

Fun fact: Stephen was the first person to be martyred for being a Christian.

# Comfort

**Definition:** A freedom from worry or disappointment.

When something bad happens, we have family and friends to help us feel better. They tell us everything will be okay and we know, through their caring and love, it will be. Jesus provides comfort and healing to those in need. Jesus tells us to never be afraid because he is always with us. What a great comfort to know He is always there!

**Jeremiah 8:18** God, you are my comfort when I am very sad. You are my comfort when I'm afraid.

How do you give comfort to others?

Fun fact: Matthias was chosen to replace Judas as an apostle.

# Commandment

**Definition:** A divine rule, especially one of the Ten Commandments.

God gave His law for our good. His 10 Commandments are not just for one group of people or one age group. They can be helpful to kids and adults. And if we break these good laws, we will have bad results. The 10 Commandments show us how to love God. He made us, and He loves us deeply.

**Matthew 22:37** Jesus answered, "Love the Lord your God with all your heart, soul and mind."

Can you list the other Commandments?

Fun fact: In regards to material possessions, Jesus taught not to be greedy. A person's life does not consist of what he owns.

# Compassion

**Definition:** Investing whatever is necessary to heal the hurts of others.

When you see someone homeless on the side of the road, do you feel compassion for them? Jesus had compassion for everyone.

**1 John 3:17** If anyone has material possessions and sees a brother or sister in need but has no pity on them, how can the love of God be in that person?

How do you show compassion?

Fun fact: The New Testament is written in the Greek Language.

# Confidence

**Definition:** A feeling of self-assurance arising from one's appreciation of one's own abilities or qualities.

We don't always have confidence, but we can develop it over time. As we learn new things, we can become better at the task and be able to perform it well.

**Hebrews 10:35** So do not throw away your confidence; it will be richly rewarded.

What area are you most confident in?

Fun fact: The Word of God is the Spirit's sword.

# Contentment

**Definition:** Realizing that God has provided everything I need for my present happiness.

Society has told us that we must have more. Not matter how many "toys" we have, we must have more. God will provide your needs. Trust God.

**1 Timothy 6:8** But if we have food and clothing, we will be content with that.

Are you content with what you have?

Fun fact: The Bible is the inspired Word of God and is His revelation to people of himself and His plan of salvation.

# Courage

**Definition:** The ability to do something that scares you.

Do you have the courage to stand up to others for something you really believe in?

Joshua is a good example of one with great courage. Joshua will forever be remembered for following God fully. His life was a demonstration that God's way truly works.

**Deuteronomy 31:6** Be strong and courageous. Do not be afraid or terrified because of them, for the LORD your God goes with you; he will never leave you or forget you.

When was a time you showed courage? (Draw or write in space below)

Fun fact: It took approximately 1600 years to write the Bible.

# Creativity

**Definition:** Approaching a need, a task, an idea from a new perspective.

Do you like doing crafts? Making new things? Determining a new way to do things? Try something new!

**Romans 12:2** Do not conform to the pattern of this world, but be transformed by the renewing of your mind. Then you will be able to test and approve what God's will is—his good, pleasing and perfect will.

How are you creative?

Fun fact: There are 39 books in the Old Testament.

# Decisiveness

**Definition:** The ability to finalize difficult decisions based on the will and ways of God.

Decisions are a part of life. We decide what to wear every day. We decide what to eat. What do you base your decisions on? Do you follow the crowd, or are you the leader of the pack?

**James 1:5** If any of you lacks wisdom, you should ask God, who gives generously to all without finding fault, and it will be given to you.

How do you decide what is right?

Fun fact: There are twenty-seven books in the New Testament.

# Dependability

**Definition:** Fulfilling what I consented to do even if it means unexpected sacrifice.

Isn't it great we have people in our life that we can depend on? We can always depend on God.

**Psalms 15:4** He must not respect hateful people. He must honor those who honor the Lord. He must keep his promises to his neighbor, even when it hurts.

Name one way you are dependable.

Fun fact: Matthew, Mark, Luke and John are the four Gospels.

# Determination

**Definition:** Purposing to accomplish God's goals in God's time regardless of the opposition.

If you are going somewhere fun, aren't you determined to get your chores done so you can go? We can do all things through God.

**2 Timothy 4:7** I have fought the good fight, I have finished the race, I have kept the faith.

How determined are you to bring your friends to God?

Fun fact: The word "gospel" means good news.

# Difference

**Definition:** A point or way in which people or things are not the same.

We live in a world where there is a lot of arguing and complaining and where there are many people who do not live like God wants us to live. Paul tells us that we need to be different than the others. We need to stop complaining and arguing so our life can shine brightly like the stars in the universe.

**Philippians 2: 14-15** Do everything without complaining or arguing. Then you will be innocent and without anything wrong in you. You will be God's children without fault.

How do you handle differences you have with others?

Fun fact: The book of Genesis tells about the beginnings of the world.

# Diligence

**Definition:** Visualizing each task as a special assignment from the Lord and using all my energies to accomplish it.

Diligence is similar to being determined. You have to work hard and steady to get the job done.

**Colossians 3:23** Whatever you do, work at it with all your heart, as working for the Lord, not for human masters.

Name one way you are diligent in your work for the Lord.

Fun fact: Acts tells about the beginnings of the Church.

# Discernment

**Definition:** The God-given ability to understand why things happen.

We don't always understand why things happen, especially when something bad happens to someone good.

**1 Samuel 16:7** But the LORD said to Samuel, "Do not consider his appearance or his height, for I have rejected him. The LORD does not look at the things people look at. People look at the outward appearance, but the LORD looks at the heart.

When you don't understand something, what do you do?

Fun fact: Psalms is the Old Testament book that is a collection of hymns and songs.

# Disciple

**Definition:** A personal follower of Jesus during his life, especially one of the twelve Apostles.

Jesus has given us a great mission to accomplish. We call it a commission because it is not a mission that we do alone. It is a mission that we do together with God. The mission is an exciting one! We have the mission to bring an eternal difference to others by sharing Jesus with them.

**Matthew 28:19** So go and make followers of all people in the world. Baptize them in the name of the Father and the Son and the Holy Spirit.

Are you willing to go on a mission with God to bring people to Jesus?

Fun fact: The Good Samaritan helped the man who had been beaten and robbed.

# Discretion

**Definition:** The ability to avoid words, actions, and attitudes which could result in undesirable consequences.

When you do something wrong, you may not want others to know. It is your decision (discretion) to tell others or not.

**Proverbs 22:3** When a wise person sees danger ahead, he avoids it. But a foolish person keeps going and gets into trouble.

When someone tells you a secret, do you tell others?

Fun fact: King David wrote many of the Psalms.

# Discover

**Definition:** Find (something or someone) unexpectedly or in the course of a search.

It's fun to explore new things. It keeps your imagination going. How much fun it is to discover something we never knew or saw before!

**Psalms 44:20-21** If we had forgotten the name of our God or spread out our hands to a foreign god, would not God have discovered it, since he knows the secrets of the heart?

What have you discovered about yourself lately?

Fun fact: An apostle is a special messenger sent by God.

# Dream

**Definition:** A series of thoughts, images, and sensations in a person's mind during sleep.

We all have a dream of what life should look like. We have dreams of what we want to be when we grow up. Never give up on your dreams.

**Genesis 41:11** Each of us had a dream the same night, and each dream had a meaning of its own.

What is the best dream you can remember?

Fun fact: We love God because He first loved us.

# Empowered

**Definition:** Having the authority or power to do something.

When we go to Church and listen to the Word, we are empowered to do what God tells us to do. Jesus wants to give us that power every day. You can do that by reading the Bible.

**Luke 9:1** Jesus called the 12 apostles together. He gave them power to heal sicknesses and power over all demons.

What are you empowered to do?

Fun fact: Peter, James, and John were three of the disciples that were Jesus' closest friends.

# Endurance

**Definition:** The inward strength to withstand stress to accomplish God's best.

Sometimes we have to do things that we don't want to do. We may have to put up with something bad in order to get something good.

**Galatians 6:9** We must not become tired of doing good. We will receive our harvest of eternal life at the right time. We must not give up!

Who gives you the strength to keep going when you are tired?

Fun fact: An epistle is a letter sent by an apostle.

# Energy

**Definition:** The strength and vitality required for sustained physical or mental activity.

Isn't it great to have energy every day to run around and play? Are we always full of energy? What about when we don't eat right. Do we still have energy to play? Maybe…maybe not.

**Colossians 1:29** To do this, I work and struggle, using Christ's great strength that works so powerfully in me.

What gives you energy?

Fun fact: Zacchaeus climbed a tree in order to see Jesus.

# Enthusiasm

**Definition:** Expressing with my soul the joy of my spirit. To be overly excited about something.

I like watching cheerleaders at football games. They have so much spirit. Their enthusiasm is contagious. They get everyone in the audience to participate in the fun!

**1 Thessalonians 5:16** Always be happy.

What gets you excited?

Fun fact: The longest book of the Bible is Psalms.

# Epiphany

**Definition:** An inspiration or divine manifestation; discovery or realization.

You want to buy your friend a nice gift but you are unsure what to buy. All of a sudden, a thought pops into your head that they really like stuffed animals. That's an example of an epiphany. Epiphany in biblical terms is: a festival celebrating Christ's appearance to the Gentiles, observed every year on January 6.

**Ephesians 3:3** God let me know his secret plan. He showed it to me. I have already written a little about this.

Share your story about an epiphany you had.

Fun fact: Jesus proved His power over nature by calming a storm on the Sea of Galilee.

# Eternal

**Definition:** Lasting or existing forever; without end or beginning.

God wants to give you eternal life in the most wonderful place called heaven. He has made heaven a special place for everyone who believes in Jesus. The Bible says heaven is a beautiful place filled with love, beauty, and, best of all, God.

**John 3:15** Then everyone who believes in him can have eternal life.

Draw a picture of what you think heaven looks like.

Fun fact: John the Baptist baptized Jesus in the Jordan River.

# Example

**Definition**: A person or thing regarded in terms of their likelihood of being imitated.

It is important for us to live our lives as examples for everyone. Take, for example, the story of Shadrach, Meshach, and Abednego. Their courage and devotion to God turned the heart of a king and an entire nation of people.

**Matthew 5:16** In the same way, you should be a light for other people. Live so that they will see the good things you do. Live so that they will praise your Father in heaven.

When things get tough, when you get frustrated or scared, how will you react?

Fun fact:  Herod was king over Judea when Jesus was born.

# Faith

**Definition:** Visualizing what God intends to do in a given situation and acting in harmony with it.

When we trust someone, we are putting our faith in them. We pray they will not let us down. Put your faith in God. God will never let you down.

**Hebrews 11:1** Now faith is confidence in what we hope for and assurance about what we do not see.

How do you describe Faith?

Fun fact: Psalms 117 is the shortest chapter in the Bible.

# Fallible

**Definition:** Capable of making mistakes or being in error.

Have you ever had a science experiment go wrong? The data that you used was incorrect making the experiment fallible. No one and nothings perfect, except for God. Therefore, we are all fallible.

**Romans 3:23-24** All people have sinned and are not good enough for God's glory. People are made right with God by his grace, which is a free gift. They are made right with God by being made free from sin through Jesus Christ.

What have you tried in the past and failed at doing?

Fun fact: Shepherds and Wise men were the two groups of men that worshipped the Christ child.

# Family

**Definition:** A group consisting of parents and children living together in a household.

Being part of a family helps us feel loved and protected. Sometimes we might feel like we have to always be good to be part of the family. God is willing to accept us into his family just the way we are. He does not expect us to be perfect. He just loves us.

**Romans 5:8** But Christ died for us while we were still sinners. In this way God shows his great love for us.

Draw a picture of your family.

Fun fact: The angel Gabriel told Mary she would be the mother of the Messiah.

# Fearless

**Definition:** Not having an unpleasant emotion caused by the belief that someone or something is dangerous, likely to cause pain, or a threat.

Can you imagine being thrown into a lions' den? Many people would have been terrified. Not Daniel. He knew God would protect him.

**Daniel 6:16** [16] So the king gave the order, and they brought Daniel and threw him into the lions' den. The king said to Daniel, "May the God you serve all the time save you!"

How does God protect us?

Fun fact: God established a feast called Passover to remember the Israelites' deliverance from Egypt.

# Flexibility

**Definition:** Not setting my affections on ideas or plans which could be changed by God or Others.

Sometimes plans change. We need to be able to change with the plans. Being flexible is part of life.

**Colossians 3:2** Set your minds on things above, not on earthly things.

When you don't agree with someone, what do you do?

Fun fact: Psalms 119 is the longest chapter of the Bible.

# Forever

**Definition:** For all future time; for always.

Jesus promises that he will not leave us as orphans. Even if we don't have an earthly father, Jesus promises that he will be our "Forever Father." He will be our Father who will always provide for our needs and comfort us when we cry. All we need to do is ask him to be our Forever Father, our Savior, the King of our heart and he will embrace us as his own child.

**John 14:18** I will not leave you as orphans; I will come to you.

Who do you know who does not have Jesus as their heavenly Father?

Fun fact: Joseph was sold as a slave in Egypt.

# Forgiveness

**Definition:** Clearing the record of those who have wronged me and allowing God to love them through me.

When people do something wrong towards us, it is sometimes not easy to forget what they did. God forgives us of our sins and he wants us to forgive others.

**Ephesians 4:32** Be kind and compassionate to one another, forgiving each other, just as in Christ God forgave you.

Name one time when you forgave someone for something they did.

Fun fact: Adam and Eve were the first man and the first woman.

# Friend

**Definition:** a person who has a strong liking for and trust in another person

God intended us to have relationships with others so that we would not be alone. He wants us to have "soul friend-ships"—aka friends who help with our spiritual develop-ment. Isn't it nice to have someone we trust and someone to talk to when we are happy or sad? That's what friends are for!

**Proverbs 18:24** Some friends may ruin you. But a real friend will be more loyal than a brother.

Who is your best friend?

Fun fact: Lot was Abraham's nephew.

# Generosity

**Definition:** Realizing that all I have belongs to God and using it for His purposes.

God loves a cheerful giver. The Bible says we are to give 10% of what we earn as a tithe to the Church. The next time you make some extra money, don't forget to give generously!

**2 Corinthians 9:6** Remember this: The person who plants a little will have a small harvest. But the person who plants a lot will have a big harvest.

Name one item you gave to someone who didn't have something.

Fun fact: God sent a flood upon the earth because people were so wicked that they thought about evil all the time.

# Gentleness

**Definition:** Showing personal care and concern in meeting the need of others.

When we hold a baby, we need to be gentle. When we pet a puppy, we have to be gentle. We want to treat others special, so they will treat us special.

**1 Thessalonians 2:7** Instead, we were like young children among you.

Name one way you can help someone in need.

Fun fact: God spared Noah and his family from the Great Flood.

# Golden Rule

**Definition:** A basic principle that should always be followed to ensure success in general, or in a particular activity.

The Golden Rule states that you should do to others as you would want them to do to you. The same thing applies to how we witness to others. The Scripture tells us to keep Christ in our heart and honor him, which is very important. It also states we must defend keeping Christ in our heart but in a way that is gentle and respectful.

**1 Peter 3:15** But respect Christ as the Lord in your hearts. Always be ready to answer everyone who asks you to explain about the hope you have.

How can you use the Golden Rule at school?

Fun fact: Methuselah lived longer than any other person. He lived 969 years.

# Gospel

**Definition**: The record of Jesus' life and teaching in the first four books of the New Testament.

Many front covers of the Bible say "The Good News." The information in the pages of the Bible is the good news and that was the reason for the title. If the Bible is the good news for everyone, then we should tell them, right? The truth of the gospel needs to be told to everyone.

**John 3:16** For God loved the world so much that he gave his only Son. God gave his Son so that whoever believes in him may not be lost, but have eternal life.

Make a list below of people you can share the gospel with.

Fun fact: Judas Iscariot is the apostle who betrayed Jesus.

# Grace

**Definition:** An attitude to kindness and compassion

We offer grace to people in our lives when we choose to respond with a kind word instead of being cruel. When someone is mean to us it is very easy to be mean back. Even if someone deserves a mean word, that is where grace comes in and gives them kindness.

**Ephesians 2:8** I mean that you have been saved by grace because you believe. You did not save yourselves. It was a gift from God.

Name a time when you didn't show someone else grace.

Fun fact: The people asked Pilate to spare the life of Barabbas instead of Jesus.

# Gratefulness

**Definition:** Making known to God and others in what ways they have benefited my life.

When someone does something nice for us, we are thankful (grateful). Our parents and grandparents are always doing something nice, so show your gratefulness with love.

**1 Corinthians 4:7** For who makes you different from anyone else? What do you have that you did not receive? And if you did receive it, why do you boast as though you did not?

Name one thing you are grateful for.

Fun fact: Shem, Ham, and Japheth were the three sons of Noah.

# Greatness

**Definition**: The quality of being of an extent, amount, or intensity considerably above the normal or average.

David's greatness started in his heart as a boy. God did not look at the boy David and say "I will make him into a king"; God looked at David and saw a king inside the boy! Your greatness starts in your heart right now. It starts with making the decision to desire to please God and doing it.

**Psalms 150:2** Praise him for his strength. Praise him for his greatness.

Inside every girl and boy is the potential of greatness when their heart is one that desires to please God. Name some ways you desire to please God?

Fun fact: Judas showed the soldiers who Jesus was by giving him a kiss on the cheek.

# Guidance

**Definition:** Advice or information aimed at resolving a problem or difficulty, especially as given by someone in authority.

As children, you are surrounded by people who are willing to give you guidance to keep you on the right path. You just have to ask!

**Proverbs 24:6** So you need the advice of others when you go to war. If you have many people to give advice, you will win.

Who do you go to for the most advice or guidance?

Fun fact: Faith is belief and complete trust in God.

# Healing

**Definition:** The process of making or becoming sound or healthy again.

Have you ever been sick? How did you feel once you were healed? Healing may sometimes take longer than we want, but when we pray for healing, God listens.

**Proverbs 12:18** The words of the reckless pierce like swords, but the tongue of the wise brings healing.

In what area of your life could you use healing?

Fun fact: Righteousness is the breastplate in Christian's armor.

# Holy Spirit

**Definition:** The third person of the trinity of God.

An egg has three parts: the shell, (crack open), the yolk (yellow stuff), and the white stuff. It has three parts, but it is still one egg. God is three persons in one. God is the Father, the Son Jesus, and the Holy Spirit. But he is still one God.

**Titus 3:6** God poured out to us the Holy Spirit fully through Jesus Christ our Savior.

What have you learned about who the Holy Spirit is?

Fun fact: Cornelius was the Roman officer who sent for Peter to come and preach for him.

# Honor

**Definition:** High respect; great esteem.

When we make a pledge with someone, we might say "on my honor I will…". When we keep that promise or pledge it shows great respect.

**Deuteronomy 5:16** Honor your father and your mother. The Lord your God has commanded you to do this. Then you will live a long time. And things will go well for you in the land. The Lord your God is going to give you this land.

Who else should you honor other than your father and mother?

Fun fact: Mary Magdalene was the first person to see Jesus after He was resurrected.

# Hope

**Definition:** A feeling of expectation and desire for a certain thing to happen.

We all have hopes and dreams. We hope we will pass a test. Hope to get picked for a team. Never let your hope die.

**Psalms 9:18** Those who have troubles will not be forgotten. The hopes of the poor will not die.

What is your biggest hope right now?

Fun fact: The gift given to the Church on the Day of Pentecost was the gift of the Holy Spirit.

# Hospitality

**Definition:** Cheerfully sharing food, shelter, and spiritual refreshment with those whom God brings into my life.

When we have friends or family come stay at our house, we want to make them feel welcome so we show them hospitality.

**Hebrews 13:2** Do not forget to show hospitality to strangers, for by so doing some people have shown hospitality to angels without knowing it.

Name one way to show hospitality.

Fun fact: It rained for forty days and nights during the Flood.

# Humility

**Definition:** Recognizing that it is actually God and others who are responsible for the achievements in my life.

We all want to take the credit for doing good. But we need to remember who got us there. It isn't always our own doing, so we need to humble ourselves.

**James 4:6** But he gives us more grace. That is why Scripture says: "God opposes the proud but shows favor to the humble.

Instead of bragging about our accomplishments, what should we do?

Fun fact: Sarah was Abraham's wife.

# Imagination

**Definition:** The ability of the mind to be creative or re-sourceful.

As kids, we love to "pretend play." Each one of us is born with the power of imagination. We can use our imagination to be creative and resourceful to create the ideal life. We can use the power of our imagination to dream, create goals, and envision our future.

**2 Corinthians 4:18** We look not at what can be seen but at what cannot be seen.

What are your dreams and goals for your future?

Fun fact: Canaan was the original name of the country God promised to Abraham.

# Jesus Love Me

**Definition:** An intense feeling of affection from Jesus.

Sometimes adults get busy and kids might even feel like they are not being treated kindly or that they are being bounced from place to place. Jesus is never too busy for you, and he wants you to feel that you can come to him in prayer anytime. He wants nothing to keep you from him.

**Mark 10: 13-16:** Some people brought their small children to Jesus so he could touch them. But his followers told the people to stop brining their children to him. When Jesus saw this, he was displeased. He said to them, "Let the little children come to me. Don't stop them. The kingdom of God belongs to people who are like these little children. I tell you the truth. You must accept the kingdom of God as a little child accepts things, or you will never enter it." Then Jesus took the children in his arms. He put his hands on them and blessed them.

Draw a picture of Jesus and you.

Fun fact: Jeremiah was called the weeping prophet.

# Initiative

**Definition:** Recognizing and doing what needs to be done before I am asked to do it.

When it is chore time, does someone need to remind you? Do you have a checklist? Or, does someone have to constantly remind you? Next time, take initiative and do them without being told.

**Romans 12:21** Do not be overcome by evil, but overcome evil with good.

Name one thing you do without someone having to ask you or remind you.

Fun fact: Melchizedek was the Priest of God and King of Salem.

# Joy

**Definition:** A feeling of great pleasure and happiness

Have you ever heard the song that goes: "I've got that joy, joy, joy, joy down in my heart"? What a great song! If you don't know the song, ask your Pastor!

Paul wrote the "Book of Joy," Philippians from jail. Imagine having so much joy while being in jail that you write about it.

**Philippians 4:4** Be full of joy in the Lord always. I will say again, be full of joy.

What gives you joy?

Fun fact: There are two divisions of the Bible, the Old Testament and the New Testament.

# Justice

**Definition:** Personal responsibility to God's unchanging laws.

We watch court dramas on TV. Do the good guys always get justice? Not always. We must encourage each other to do what is right.

**Micah 6:8** The Lord has told you what is good. He has told you what he wants from you: Do what is right to other people. Love being kind to others. And live humbly, trusting your God.

Did you ever have a situation happen and felt you didn't get justice?

Fun fact: Ishmael was the name of the son born to Abraham and Hagar.

# Kindness

**Definition:** The quality of being friendly, generous, and considerate.

Jesus wants us to be kind to others. He wants us to be just like him. He never said it would always be easy.

**Galatians 5:22** But the fruit of the Spirit is love, joy, peace, patience, kindness, goodness, faithfulness, gentleness and self-control.

How can you show kindness to others?

Fun fact: Revelation is the New Testament book that is composed almost entirely of prophecies.

# Let Go, Let God

**Definition:** To stop trying to do things on your own and allow God to have control.

When we try to rush to accomplish a goal, we have obstacles that get in our way. The harder we work, the more obstacles we encounter. We need to remember we are not alone. We need to make the decision to let go and let God. Letting go brings a fresh outlook to our goals. He is here to help – let him!

**Jeremiah 42:3** So pray that the Lord your God will tell us where we should go. And pray he will tell us what we should do.

What area of your life do you need to "let go – let God?"

Fun fact: Babylon was the city where many people were taken as captives.

# Listen

**Definition:** To give your full attention to a sound or voice.

God uses kids to speak important messages to adults when the kids are willing to spend time with the Lord in prayer and when they have a heart that says, "Here I am Lord! I want to listen to you!"

**1 Samuel 3:10** The Lord came and stood there. He called as he had before. He said, "Samuel, Samuel!" Samuel said, "Speak, Lord I am your servant, and I am listening."

Is God telling you to tell an adult that is going through a hard time that God loves them and he can help?

Fun fact: Hezekiah was who God gave a sign of the sun moving backwards to show him that he was being healed.

# Lost

**Definition:** Unable to find one's way; not knowing one's whereabouts.

Have you even known someone who stole things from a store? This is bad since stealing is a sin and against the law. Remember that no one is truly lost to sin. Everyone can be saved, so pray for them that God would change them so that their soul is not lost forever.

**Romans 6:23** The payment for sin is death. But God gives us the free gift of life forever in Christ Jesus our Lord.

Do you know a friend that is lost? How can you help them?

Fun fact: Elisha was the prophet that succeeded Elijah.

# Love

**Definition:** Giving to others' basic needs without having as my motive personal reward.

Jesus says it is most important to love God with everything in us. Everything we do, think, and say should come from our love of God. Then our love for God will spill over to everyone around us. When they see God's love through us, it will help them begin a relationship with him.

**1 Corinthians 13:4** Love is patient and kind. Love is not jealous, it does not brag, and it is not proud.

How can you show your love for God and others?

Fun fact: Moses was the baby that Pharaoh's daughter found floating in the river.

# Loyalty

**Definition:** Using difficult times to demonstrate my commitment to God and to those whom He has called me to serve.

Being a loyal friend is a good quality. Being there for someone in good times and bad times is a loving gesture.

**John 15:13** Greater love has no one than this: to lay down one's life for one's friends.

How are you a loyal friend?

Fun fact: Moses fled from Egypt because it was known that he had killed an Egyptian who mistreated an Israelite.

# Meekness

**Definition:** Surrendering my personal rights and expectations to God.

When we refer to someone as meek, they are usually shy. Being meek is not a weakness.

**Psalms 62:5** Yes, my soul, find rest in God; my hope comes from him.

Name one time it was best you kept quiet and didn't say anything.

Fun fact: God appeared to Moses out of the burning bush at Mount Horeb (Mount Sinai).

# Mercy

**Definition:** Kind and forgiving treatment of someone.

Compassion leads you to have mercy, which is like for-giveness. When someone commits a crime, they might ask the judge to have mercy – which means giving them a lesser punishment.

**Psalms 86:15** But Lord, you are a god who shows mercy and is kind. You don't become angry quickly. You have great love and faithfulness.

How do you share loving kindness and forgiveness to oth-ers?

Fun fact: Solomon erected the Temple of the Lord for God.

# Miracle

**Definition**: A surprising and welcome event that is not explained by natural or scientific laws and is therefore considered to be the work of a divine person or thing.

Some men carried a paralyzed man on a mat to see Jesus to get healed. When they couldn't get to Jesus, they went up on the roof and lowered him on his mat through the tiles into the middle of the crowd, right in front of Jesus. Jesus said "I tell you, get up, take your mat and go home." Immediately he stood up, took his mat and went home praising God.

**Luke 5:24** But I will prove to you that the Son of Man has authority on earth to forgive sins. So, Jesus said to the paralyzed man, "Tell you stand up! Take your mat and go home."

Would you be willing to be a good friend like that for someone? Draw a picture of your friend.

Fun fact: Solomon asked God to give him wisdom when we became king.

# Obedience

**Definition:** Freedom to be creative under the protection of divinely appointed authority.

Being able to do as you are told is a sign of obedience. It is also a way we learn from others.

**2 Corinthians 10:5** And we destroy every proud thing that raises itself against the knowledge of God. We capture every thought and make it give up and obey Christ.

Why is it important to obey your parents?

Fun fact: The parting of the red sea was the miracle that allowed Israel to leave the land of Egypt.

# Offering

**Definition:** A thing offered, especially as a gift or contribution.

At Church we take an offering to give a portion back to God because God gives us everything! Our offering goes to mission work and to help in the community. The Bible says we are to give one tenth of everything we earn. The next time you get your allowance, set aside your 10% to give back to God and see how God blesses you!

**Proverbs 3: 9** Honor the Lord by giving him part of your wealth. Give him the first fruits from all your crops.

If we don't have money to give, what else can we use as an offering to God?

Fun fact:  Saul of Tarsus went to Damascus to arrest Christians.

# Omnipotent

**Definition:** Having unlimited power.

God is omnipotent. He can give power to people when He wants to and He can take power away when He wants to. God has unlimited power. Samson was a strong man who lost his power.... true it happened because his hair was cut off, but ultimately it was because he forgot that it was God who gave him the power and God who could take it away. Samson began to believe that he was in control and forgot about God.

**Joshua 4:24** The Lord did this so all people would know he has great power. Then they will always respect the Lord your God.

Can you think of other things (stories in the Bible) that God has done with his power and might?

Fun fact: Barnabus helped Paul on his first missionary journey.

# Omnipresent

**Definition:** Existing everywhere at once.

Can you be here and on the moon? Can you be here and be in the next room? Or, can you be at the front of the room and the back of the room? God is everywhere all the time. *He is not limited by time and space.* God was in the burning bush, God was in the pillar of cloud and pillar of fire, God was in the cloud that settled on the temple. But He was also everywhere else at the same time.

**Psalms 139:7** Where can I go to get away from your Spirit? Where can I run from you?

Draw something below to help you remember God is everywhere.

Fun fact: Angels are spiritual beings created by God.

# Opportunity

**Definition:** A set of circumstances that makes it possible to do something.

God is able to use the believer in all kinds of circumstances. When we are faced with difficulties, for ourselves or others, we must recognize that God's wisdom helps us make the best decisions. We must remain humble before God and never miss the opportunity to share with others that God is the source of all wisdom.

**Luke 21:13** But this will give you an opportunity to tell about me.

Where can you share with others that God is the source of all wisdom?

Fun fact: When we say God is immutable, we mean He never changes. He is always the same.

# Orderliness

**Definition:** Preparing myself and my surroundings so I will achieve the greatest efficiency.

Do you find it hard to concentrate when the room is messy, the TV is on, the dog is barking, and your brother or sister is crying? When we keep things in order, it is easier to concentrate.

**1 Corinthians 14:40** But everything should be done in a fitting and orderly way.

Why is it important to keep your room clean?

Fun fact: God provided bread for the Israelites in the wilderness by sending manna.

# Passion

**Definition:** A strong and barely controllable emotion.

We all have something we really, really like. Things like baseball, basketball, bike riding or other activities.  We love to do them, so that means we have a passion for them. The Bible tells us that we're to seek God passionately. You are not by nature passionate about God. It's something that you must choose to do. We get distracted and everything in life tries to keep us from being passionate about God. So, He says "keep your passion going. Keep the fires going." It's a discipline. It's not just automatic.

**Mark 12:30** Love the Lord your God. Love him with all your heart, all your soul, all your mind, and all your strength.

What are you passionate about?

Fun fact: Prayer is talking to God.

# Patience

**Definition:** Accepting a difficult situation from God without giving Him a deadline to remove it.

Being patient is probably one of the hardest things we have to do. Waiting in line, waiting for a grade or a friend to come over. It all requires patience.

**Romans 5:3-4** And we also have joy with our troubles because we know that these troubles produce patience.

Name one time you didn't have patience.

Fun fact: Aaron and Hur helped Moses gain the victory over the Amalekites by holding up Moses' hand

# Peace

**Definition:** A quiet and calm state of mind. Agreement and harmony among people.

There is a song about peace that goes – Let there be peace on earth and let it begin with me. In order to have peace in our lives, it needs to start with us. Being nice to others is a great way to gain peace in your life.

**Philippians 4:7** And God's peace will keep your hearts and minds in Christ Jesus. The peace that God gives is so great that we cannot understand it.

What is another way you can create peace in your life?

Fun fact: Repentance is having a change in mind, heart and direction.

# Persuasiveness

**Definition:** Guiding vital truths around another's mental roadblocks.

Have you ever tried to win someone over? Tried to get them on your side? It takes skills to get someone to go along with you. Persuading someone to see your point of view is not always easy.

**2 Timothy 2:24** And a servant of the Lord must not quarrel! He must be kind to everyone. He must be a good teacher. He must be patient.

How do you get others on your side?

Fun fact: God gave Moses the Ten Commandments on Mount Sinai.

# Potential

**Definition:** Having or showing the capacity to become or develop into something in the future.

Has someone ever told you "you have potential?" That means they can see you doing something great.

**Joshua 1:5** Just as I was with Moses, so I will be with you. No one will be able to stop you all your life. I will not leave you. I will never leave you alone.

How do you build up your own potential?

Fun fact: Readiness (preparation) that comes from the gospel of peace is part of Christian armor and is what is worn on the feet.

# Power

**Definition:** The ability to do something or act in a particular way.

Did you know the Bible gives us power? The Word of God is the strongest thing we have against Satan.

**Deuteronomy 34:12** For no one has ever shown the mighty power or performed the awesome deeds that Moses did in the sight of all Israel.

If you could have super powers, what would they be?

Fun fact: Those who hear Jesus's teachings but do not do them are like the foolish man who builds his house upon sand.

# Pray for Others

**Definition:** Address a request or expression of thanks to God for another person.

There is a saying that goes: If we help others to get what they want we can then get what we want. Praying for others is one way to do this.

**James 5:16** Therefore confess your sins to each other and pray for each other so that you may be healed. The prayer of a righteous person is powerful and effective.

How often should you pray for others?

Fun fact: The tent makers who assisted Paul at Corinth were Aquila and Priscilla.

# Problem

**Definition:** A matter or situation regarded as unwelcome or harmful and needing to be dealt with and overcome.

Sometimes we have small problems and other times we have what we think are big problems. People with any size problem need God.

**Psalms 62:8** People, trust God all the time. Tell him all your problems. God is our protection.

Who do you go to when you have a problem?

Fun fact: Grace means that God offers us His love and forgiveness as a gift and not because we earned it or deserve it.

# Punctuality

**Definition:** Showing high esteem for other people and their time.

There are some people that hate being late going somewhere. There are other people that are just late to everything. Being on-time is a sign of respect for other's time.

**Ecclesiastes 3:1** There is a time for everything. Everything on earth has its special season.

Why is it important to be on time?

Fun fact: You shall have no other Gods before me is the first of the Ten Commandments.

# Reality

**Definition:** The world or the state of things as they actually exist.

We live in a world where reality is sometimes hard to understand. We must live according to the Bible to keep in the reality Jesus wants us to live.

**Colossians 2:17** In the past, these things were like a shadow of what was to come. But the new things that were coming are found in Christ.

How do you feel about the way our world is today?

Fun fact: Peter escaped from prison the night before Herod planned to kill him by an angel opening the prison for him.

# Relationships

**Definition:** The way in which two or more concepts, objects or people are connected, or the state of being connected.

Without relationships, we would be very lonely. Jesus wants us to have friends. He wants us to have relationships with each other and talk about him daily.

**Philippians 2:5** In your relationships with one another, have the same mindset as Christ Jesus

Are you acting like Jesus in your relationship with others?

Fun fact: In Ephesians, Paul commands all children to obey your parents.

# Repent

**Definition:** To feel or express sincere regret or remorse about one's wrongdoing or sin.

We have all done something bad in our life. When we realized we have sinned, we need to apologize and ask for forgiveness. Then we need to make it right. God always forgives. Just make sure you learn from your mistake and not do it again!

**Matthew 3:8** You must do the things that show that you have really changed your heart and lives.

If you have done something wrong to someone lately, did you repent? How?

Fun fact: Justification means when we accept Jesus as our Savior, God accepts us as we have not sinned.

# Resourcefulness

**Definition:** Wise use of that which others would normally overlook or discard.

There may be a time we may not have the supplies to finish our project so we start looking around to find something that may work. This is being resourceful.

**Luke 16:10** Whoever can be trusted with very little can also be trusted with much, and whoever is dishonest with very little will also be dishonest with much.

How do you bless others with what you have?

Fun fact: You shall not misuse the name of the Lord your God is one of the Ten Commandments that doesn't allow cursing and swearing.

# Responsibility

**Definition:** Knowing and doing what both God and others are expecting from me.

Being responsible for something is a great task. We are responsible to spread the word of God to others.

**Romans 14:12** So then, each of us will give an account of ourselves to God.

What is one of your responsibilities at home?

Fun fact: Paul called the first commandment with promise "Honor your father and your mother."

# Revelation

**Definition:** The act of making something evident; uncover or unveil.

A revelation is when your friend who has always had three dogs and suddenly tells you he is a cat person. Another great example is: an engineer was watching his son play with blocks and he had a sudden revelation on how to fix his construction problem.

**Revelation 1:1** This is the revelation of Jesus Christ. God gave this revelation to Jesus, to show his servants what must soon happen. And Jesus sent his angel to show it to his servant John.

Share a revelation you have had:

Fun fact: God gave the law to show all people what sin is.

# Reverence

**Definition:** Awareness of how God is working through the people and events in my life to produce the character of Christ in me.

An example of a reverent person is someone who constantly gives thanks and praise to God.

**Proverbs 23:17** Don't envy sinners. But always respect the Lord.

How do you thank God for what you have?

Fun fact: "You shall not steal" is one of the Ten Commandments that protects our right to own possessions.

# Righteous

**Definition:** A person or conduct which is morally right and justifiable.

Being righteous literally means to be right, especially in a moral way. Religious people often talk about being righteous. In their view, the righteous person not only does the right thing for other people but also follows the laws of their religion.

**Luke 1:75** We will be righteous and holy before God as long as we live.

What is a time you did the right thing for someone?

Fun fact: Thomas was the first disciple who doubted Jesus' resurrection.

# Salvation

**Definition:** Salvation means being saved from certain death.

Salvation is not a reward for the good we have done, so none of us can take any credit for it. Remember a gift is something someone else gives to you. You can't buy it, or do anything to deserve it. By believing and trusting in Jesus because he died for your sins on the cross, you can have the gift of eternal life (salvation).

**Romans 6:23** The payment for sin is death. But God gives us the free gift of a life forever in Christ Jesus our Lord.

Have you asked Jesus to be your Savior?

Fun fact: Exodus 20:16 prohibits lying. "You shall not give false testimony against your neighbor."

# Scapegoat

**Definition:** Someone who is punished for the errors of others.

When someone gets caught lying or doing something wrong, they might use their friend as a scapegoat. Somehow the wrong doing will end up the friend's fault. It is hard to own up to our own mistakes, but we must in order to learn from them.

**Leviticus 16:22** So the goat will carry all the people's sins on itself. It will go to a lonely place in the desert. The man who leads the goat will let it loose there.

Have you ever used someone as a scapegoat? (Be honest!)

Fun fact: An angel rolled the stone away from the tomb for the women to get inside.

# Security

**Definition:** Structuring my life around that which is eternal and cannot be destroyed or taken away.

We all want to feel secure and safe. God will protect you in all that you do.

**John 6:27** Earthly food spoils and ruins. So, don't work to get that kind of food. But work to get the food that stays good always and gives you eternal life. The Son of Man will give you that food. God the Father has shown that he is with the Son of Man.

In what way do you feel secure in your home life?

Fun fact: Exodus (chapter) 20 is the book and chapter of the Bible that we find the first record of the Ten Commandments.

# Self-Control

**Definition:** Instant obedience to the initial promptings of God's Spirit.

When something happens around you, are you able to control your reactions? When someone falls, do you laugh? Or, do you control yourself and make sure they are okay?

**Galatians 5:24-25** Those who belong to Christ Jesus have crucified their own sinful selves. They have given up their old selfish feelings and the evil things they wanted to do. We get our new life from the Spirit. So, we should follow the Spirit.

Name one time you didn't have self-control.

Fun fact: The very center of the Bible is Psalms 118:8.

# Self-Esteem

**Definition:** Confidence in one's own worth or abilities; self-respect.

Self-esteem – like confidence – is something that isn't always easy to have. We must believe in ourselves. Otherwise, how will others believe in us?

**Proverbs 1:3** They will teach you how to be wise and self-controlled. They will teach you what is honest and fair and right.

What is one area of your life where you need more self-esteem?

Fun fact: Salvation is the helmet in Christian's armor.

# Sensitivity

**Definition:** Exercising my senses so I can perceive the true spirit and emotions of those around me.

When something bothers you, find someone to talk to. If you don't talk about the situation you may become sensitive to it and not ever want to talk about it.

**Romans 12:15** Rejoice with those who rejoice; mourn with those who mourn.

Name one time you hurt someone else's feelings and didn't mean to.

Fun fact: Moses saw the Promised Land from the mountain of Nebo.

# Serenity

**Definition:** The state of being calm, peaceful and untroubled.

Many people go to the beach to relax. The waves at the beach have a calming effect. When you can fully relax, the presence of God is strong. No matter where we are or what is happening, we can never separate from God. God gives us the gift of serenity at all times – we just need to accept it.

**2 Thessalonians 3:16** We pray that the Lord of peace will give you peace at all times and in every way. May the Lord be with all of you.

Draw the image that comes to mind when you think of serenity.

Fun fact: Joab was captain of David's army.

# Sin

**Definition:** An action that breaks a religious law.

We all sin each and every day. From a small little lie, being mean to others, or watching a TV show we know doesn't follow a Christian life. It is important that we learn from our sin and do not continue to do the same bad behaviors that make God sad.

**1 John 5:17** Doing wrong is always sin. But there is sin that does not lead to eternal death.

Make a list of what you think are sins.

Fun fact: The Israelites wandered in the wilderness for forty years.

# Sharing

**Definition:** Have a portion of something with another or others.

When we are young, we really don't like to share. As we grow older, we learn to share. Sharing is caring.

**Philippians 2:1-2** Does your life in Christ give you strength? Does his love comfort you? Do we share together in the Spirit? Do you have mercy and kindness?

How often do you share your love for God with others?

Fun fact: Faith in Christian's armor is our shield.

# Sincerity

**Definition:** Eagerness to do what is right with transparent motives.

When you go out of your way to do something nice for someone, you are being sincere in your actions. You don't expect a reward.

**1 Peter 1:22** Now that you have purified yourselves by obeying the truth so that you have sincere love for each other, love one another deeply, from the heart.

Do you do something nice for a reward or because it is good to help others?

Fun fact: Moses was 120 years old when he died.

# Smile

**Definition:** Form one's features into a pleased, kind, or amused expression.

The best gift you can give someone is your smile. It's free and it is easy to do. Share your smile today!

**Job 29:24** I smiled at them when they doubted. And my approval was important to them.

Why is it important to smile at others?

Fun fact: Christian's should use the shield of faith to protect themselves from Satan's flaming arrows.

# Speech

**Definition:** The expression of or the ability to express thoughts and feelings by certain sounds.

Just like you would talk to your best friends and family with kindness and care, you should be prepared to use that same kindness and care with everyone. As God's witnesses to the world, we must be prepared to share God's love and gospel with gracious speech.

**Colossians 4:6** When you talk, you should always be kind and wise. Then you will be able to answer everyone in the way you should.

Draw a picture of you speaking to a crowd of people:

Fun fact: Jesus died on the cross for our sins.

# Strength

**Definition:** The quality or state of being physically strong
- He pushed the rock with all his strength

When faced with hard decisions, especially when needing to stand up for what we believe, God gives us the strength to make the right choice. Shadrach, Meshach and Abednego knew what the king was asking was wrong. And they did not hesitate to stand up for God. They believed He would protect them and give them the strength to withstand the pressure of the king. In the end, Shadrach, Meshach and Abednego were safe and God received the glory.

**Philippians 4:13** I can do all things through Christ because he gives me strength.

Name a time when you had to be really strong.

Fun fact: David ruled as a king for forty years.

# Surrender

**Definition:** A believer that completely gives up his own will and subjects his thoughts, ideas, and deeds to the will and teachings of God.

You're surrendering all the time. When you fly in an airplane, you sit down in the seat and surrender to that plane. There is nothing you can do about it. When you have surgery, you surrender to the doctors, because again there is nothing you can do about it. If you want a change in your life, if you want forgiveness and peace and joy that you've never known before, God demands total surrender. He becomes the Lord and the ruler of your life.

**Psalms 37:7** Surrender yourself to the Lord and wait patiently for him.

Have you surrendered yourself totally and unconditionally to God? Why or why not?

Fun fact: Christians should always rejoice.

# Testimony

**Definition:** Something that serves as evidence.

When you give testimony, you are telling what you saw or what you know. Your testimony that your hand was not in the cookie jar goes against the testimony of several eye witnesses! People give a testimony of how they were saved and now live for Jesus.

**Psalms 107:2** This is what the people the Lord has saved should say. They are the ones he has saved from the enemy.

What is your testimony?

Fun fact: Paul wrote two letters to Timothy which are books of the Bible.

# Thoroughness

**Definition:** Knowing what factors will diminish the effectiveness of my work or words if neglected.

Before you turn in a test at school, you check your answers. This is being thorough to make sure you didn't leave anything out.

**Proverbs 18:15** The mind of a smart person is ready to get knowledge. The wise person listens to learn more.

How important is it to finish something you start?

Fun fact: Rahab protected the spies Joshua sent to Jericho.

# Thriftiness

**Definition:** Not letting myself or others spend that which is not necessary.

We talked about saving and spending before, but it is important to mention it again. God wants us to be a cheerful giver. Not just of our money, but of our time and gifts.

**Luke 16:11** So if you have not been trustworthy in handling worldly wealth, who will trust you with true riches?

What is one thing you can save your money for that would help God?

Fun fact: Rahab marked her home with a scarlet cord in the window so she would be protected when Jericho was captured.

# Tolerance

**Definition:** Acceptance of others as unique expressions of specific character qualities in varying degrees of maturity.

When you practice accepting others beliefs, values and ways of living, you are being tolerant.

**Philippians 2:2** If so, make me very happy by having the same thoughts, sharing the same love, and having one mind and purpose.

Sometimes it is hard to tolerate weird behavior from others. Name one time you went through something difficult and didn't say anything.

Fun fact: When Samuel was a child, he heard the voice of God speak to him during the night.

# Trust

**Definition:** A belief that someone or something is reliable, good, and honest.

When God told Noah to build an ark, he trusted God and did what he was told. All of the people around Noah made fun of him and thought he was crazy, but Noah didn't care because he knew he was obeying God. In the end, it was Noah's trust in God's voice that saved him and his family from the flood.

**Proverbs 3:5** Trust in the Lord with all your heart. Don't depend on your own understanding.

Name a time when you placed all of your trust in God.

Fun fact: We love him because he first loved us.

# Truthfulness

**Definition:** Earning future trust by accurately reporting past facts.

When you do something wrong, do you tell the truth? The truth will eventually come out. The truth will set you free!

**Ephesians 4:25** Therefore each of you must put off falsehood and speak truthfully to your neighbor, for we are all members of one body.

How important is it to be truthful?

Fun fact: Goliath was the giant that David killed.

# Understanding

**Definition:** The ability to grasp mentally something; comprehend.

In many situations people didn't fully understand what Jesus was saying. There may be times you won't understand what the Bible is saying. Ask God – he is waiting for you to help you!

**Job 12:13** But God has wisdom and power. He has good advice and understanding.

Is there something you are unsure of and would like to understand?

Fun fact: Barnabas helped Paul on his first missionary journey.

# Witness

**Definition:** An open statement of one's religious faith through words or actions.

God calls us to be witnesses to his kingdom. As a witness for God's kingdom, we are called to spread the gospel and God's love. There are two major things that we can do to help make sure that we are good witnesses. First, pray and read the Bible, seeking the truth of God. Second, watch what you say and do, making sure that it is right with the Lord.

**Acts 22:15** You will be his witness to all people. You will tell them about the things you have seen and heard.

What else can you do to be a good witness for God?

Fun fact: Doctrine is teaching from the Bible.

# Wisdom

**Definition:** Seeing and responding to life's situations from God's frame of reference.

It is a characteristic of wisdom not to do desperate or crazy things. If you seek wisdom, ask God.

**Proverbs 9:10** The fear of the LORD is the beginning of wisdom, and knowledge of the Holy One is understanding.

Who do you know who is wise? What makes them wise?

Fun fact: God performed a miracle for Moses at Rephidim by bringing water from a rock.

# Worry

**Definition:**  To feel or express great concern for someone or something.

Sometimes when we take a test at school we worry if we did good or bad on the test. Or, if someone we love is sick. we may worry if they will get better soon. God wants us to give our worries to him and always give thanks for his blessings.

**Philippians 4:6** Do not worry about anything. But pray and ask God for everything you need. And when you pray, always give thanks.

What do you worry about?

Fun fact: Redemption is the price Jesus paid for our salvation.

# Worship

**Definition:** The feeling or expression of reverence and adoration for a deity. "The worship of God"

There are many ways to worship God. You can sing, pray, lift your hands high, hold your hands out to the side or hold your hands like you are holding something in front of your body. You should worship in a way that you are comfortable with - and not worry about how someone else does it. There is no right or wrong way to worship.

**Luke 1:50** God will always give mercy to those who worship him.

How do you like to worship?

Fun fact: Prayer is talking with God.

# Zeal

**Definition:** Filled with or showing a strong and energetic desire to get something done or see something succeed.

Zeal is dedication or enthusiasm for something. If you have zeal, you're willing, energized, and motivated. Zeal is often used in a religious sense, meaning devotion to God or another religious cause, like being a missionary.

**Isiah 59:17** The Lord covered himself with goodness like armor. He put on the helmet of salvation. He put on the clothes of punishment. And he put on the coat of his strong love.

Draw a picture of what the Lord looked like in Isiah 59:17.

Fun fact: Praise is expressing our love to God for all that he has done.

## About the Author

MICHELE SFAKIANOS (Sfa-can-iss) is a Registered Nurse, Certified Life Transformation Specialist, Speaker, Trainer, and Award-winning Author. Michele helps individuals live their passion and 'grow forward' in their life purpose.

As a John Maxwell Certified Coach, Teacher and Speaker, she offers workshops, seminars, keynote speaking, and coaching, aiding your personal and professional growth through study and practical application of John's proven leadership methods. Working together, Michele will move you and/or your team or organization in the desired direction to reach your goals. Her goal-oriented outlook on life and passion for helping others to unlock their full potential and live their dream life, led her to join the John Maxwell Team. She is an Award-winning and Best-Selling Author. Michele wants you to have a structured and practical plan in place to avoid becoming overwhelmed and over-stressed. She has personally used these tools to enhance her own productivity, development and decision-making skills to create a more balanced lifestyle.

www.ingramcontent.com/pod-product-compliance
Lightning Source LLC
Chambersburg PA
CBHW060506280326
41933CB00014B/2876

* 9 781732 272262 *